THE TRUMP PASSOVER HAGGADAH

"People All The Time They Come Up And Tell Me This Is The Best Haggadah They've Ever Read, They Do, Believe Me"

Written by
Dave Cowen

NOTE:

This Haggadah is read from left to right, which is how we start making Haggadahs great again.

CONTENTS

DONALD TRUMP DOES THE INTRODUCTION

DONALD TRUMP: Many people don't know this, but I have three Jewish grandchildren. They're Jewish, but they're very fine people, my grandchildren, very fine. There are fine people in many religions. Not all. But many.

My Jewish grandchildren FaceTimed me the other day, the three of them, they said, "President Zayde, President Zayde, President Zayde, are you coming to Passover this year, President Zayde?!"

I'd only ever been to one Passover. Back in 1984, when my best Jew lawyer, Roy Cohn, finally convinced me to accept one of his invitations to a Seder at his penthouse in Manhattan. Frankly, there's only one word to describe that night. *Boring.* Even with Madonna as my date, and I'm talking still-hot, pre-pregnant, pre-Kabbalah Madonna, it was unbearable. Before we could eat, we had to take turns reading from these old, raggedy, dirty— filthy really— paper manuals, these Haggadahs, right, that's what you call them? Well, let me tell you, they're very low energy, very poorly written stuff, and the whole thing went on forever, I left after the second cracker course.

I vowed I'd never go to another Seder again. And I still wouldn't consider it, even when Ivanka converted, and she and Jared recommended them to me. She and Jared have recommended a lot of stuff to me, which I check out, and end up really not agreeing with, The Paris Agreement, for one, Roy Moore's guilt, for another. But, this year, when my little Jewish grandchildren asked their President Zayde to come to their Seder, I gotta tell you, seeing their little Jew-faces, on that probably Jew-invented FaceTime, I changed my mind. But not without getting a really good deal first. I told them, "I'm a tremendous dealmaker, you know that, right, children, you know President Zayde is a tremendous dealmaker, OK?" They said they did know that, and that everyone knows that, it's very widely known. I said, "Good, so I'll come to

Passover, but I'll only come if I get to lead the Seder, OK?" They said, "You're a tremendous leader, you're the leader of the country, the leader of the free world, of course you can lead the Seder."

So off I went, and I took a billion of my many billions of dollars for the Afikomen prize, because I'm such a terrific President Zayde, to lead my first Seder. I then had it transcribed and printed as this here Haggadah, for a very reasonable price, some say too reasonable, we might have to raise the prices, we'll see. I don't know if Haggadahs were once great, and they started not being great at some point. Maybe after they started writing them from right to left, which we're not doing with this one, by the way. But I told my grandchildren, and I'm telling you, you're gonna love Trump's Haggadah. Think of Trump's Haggadah as a big play, and divide up the speaking parts amongst your guests as they come up, and you'll re-live the greatness of Trump's Seder. I have no doubt you're all gonna become more of the many many many people that all the time they come up and tell me this is the best Haggadah they've ever read, you will, believe me.

STEPHEN MILLER DOES THE REMOVAL OF THE HAMETZ

STEPHEN MILLER: Hi everyone, I'm Stephen Miller, 32 year-old Senior Policy Advisor to President Trump. I'm a Jewish man from Santa Monica, California, which, there are a lot of us there, but they're mostly the kind of Jews that are very unfair to President Trump, and, frankly, don't understand what the stablest genius I've ever met is trying to do with this country, and its illegal immigrants, who are completely different from other immigrants, like the Jews, that came and made this country great.

Analogously, our G-d, the President of the World, the Leader of the Free Universe, the Commander In Chief of the Cosmos, has instructed us to remove all Hametz from our domain. Many households informally adopt the practice of amnesty for their Hametz.

These sanctuary households contend that they don't need to remove what's not really hurting anyone, what's been in the domain for a long time, just sitting in the cabinet. They say it's beneficial to their household to keep their box of Triscuits or their package of Flour Tortillas, because those foodstuffs keep for more than 8 days, longer than the length of Passover, and then can be eaten again afterwards. I enjoy Triscuits. I don't care for Flour Tortillas.

But sanctuary households, listen up, removing Hametz is the law of the land. And the law of the land must be followed. No exceptions.

Like undocumented immigrants, all Hametz is illegal and must be removed. Technically, all should be searched for, collected, and burned. But there are some moderates at the table, who think that goes too far. I'm looking at you, Gary Cohn. And so, we say the prayer of the removal of the Hametz:

EVERYONE:

ברוך אתה יהוה אלהינו מלך
העולם אשר קדשנו במצותיו וצונו
על בעור חמץ

*Baruch atah Adonai, Eloheinu Melech ha'olam,
asher kid'shanu b'mitzvotav v'tzivanu al biur
hametz.*

*Praised Are You, Our G-d, President of the World,
Leader of the Free Universe, Commander In Chief
of the Cosmos, who blesses us with mitzvot and
instructs us to remove hametz.*

STEVEN MNUCHIN DOES THE YOM TOV CANDLE LIGHTING

STEVEN MNUCHIN: Hello there, I'm Steven Mnuchin, President Trump's Secretary of the Treasury. Also a Jewish man like Stephen Miller, but with a better spelling of the name Steven.

The Seder begins when we light the Yom Tov Candles. We do this at sundown, in order to mark a transition, from one time to another. From a regular time to a special one. For example, from the ordinary time of a 35 percent tax rate on American corporations to the better time of a 21 percent tax rate on American corporations, which will not help the poor enough today and will indebt the next generation. A time where coastal liberals are targeted to lose vital deductions, especially self-employed humor writers who make it their half-baked business to poke fun at me.

We cover our eyes, while we recite the Yom Tov Candle Lighting blessing, mostly to avoid looking at our fellow citizens, who know that our tax bill is a direct transfer of money to the rich and to corporations.

STEPHEN MILLER: Steven. Steven! Steven!!! Can I add something here, Steven?!

STEVEN MNUCHIN: Sure, Stephen, my wunderkind colleague, with an inferior spelling of our name, an inferior hairline, even though you're over 20 years younger, and an inferiority complex, which makes you shout the name of the person you're talking to.

STEPHEN MILLER: I heard that liberal rabbis say the flickering flame of the Yom Tov Candles can also remind us of the flickering flame of The Statue of Liberty, because both suggest immigration to a promised land. Those ruvs are wrong though. As we all know, The Statue of Liberty's flame is a symbol of American liberty lighting the world. It's not, as popularly misunderstood due to a poem written years later— by a woman no less— a symbol that America should take in quote, "Your tired, your poor, your huddled masses," unquote.

GARY COHN: Gary Cohn, Chief Economic Advisor. Also a Jewish man. Not named Stephen or Steven though. Wanted to add something here as well. We could actually use more of the poor, so we can tax them, to pay for the cuts for the rich and the corporations.

STEPHEN MILLER: Cohn. Cohn! Cohn!!! Just when I thought your ideas couldn't get any more secretly moderate, you say that, and totally redeem yourself!

KELLYANNE CONWAY: Kellyanne Conway, Counselor to the President. Not a Jew. Not a man. Just wanted to add, according to Jewish law, a woman is supposed to light the candles...

STEVEN MNUCHIN: Is that one of your "alternative facts," shiksa?

GARY COHN: Not falling for one of those, shiksa.

STEPHEN MILLER: Shiksa! Shiksa!!!
Shiksa!!!!!! Who do you think we are, the media?!
Let's read the prayer, Jew Boyz!

EVERYONE:

בָּרוּךְ אַתָּה אֲדֹנָי אֱלֹהֵינוּ מֶלֶךְ
הָעוֹלָם אֲשֶׁר קִדְּשָׁנוּ בְּמִצְוֹתָיו וְצִוָּנוּ
לְהַדְלִיק נֵר שֶׁל [שַׁבָּת וְשֶׁל] יוֹם טוֹ

Baruch atah Adonai, Eloheinu Melech ha'olam,
asher kid'shanu b'mitzvotav v'tzivanu l'hadlik ner
shel Yom Tov.

Praised Are You, Our G-d, President Of The World,
Leader of the Free Universe, Commander In Chief
of the Cosmos, Without A Term Limit, who blesses
us with mitzvot and instructs us to ignite the lights
of the festival day.

MELANIA TRUMP DOES THE SEDER TABLE

MELANIA TRUMP: Melania here, and wow, am I really still FLOTUS? I keep thinking one day I'll wake up and this will all have been a bad dream. Alas, even though my husband *looks* like the imaginary, orange troll-monster we use to scare children in mother Slovenia, unfortunately this is no fairy tale. So, someone pass me a bottle of Xanax— that's kosher, right?— and let's set the Seder table!

According to these instructions, the first thing I must do is display the best utensils and glassware to make the table look as luxurious as possible. Well, the Trumps can certainly do that! Our gold-plated cutlery will go perfectly with the gold-colored curtains and solid-gold toilets. Next, we need cushions at each seat for reclining. We already do that, too! Donald likes to eat his meals on the couch, while getting debriefed by *Fox & Friends*.

Now I must move on to the Seder Plate. First, we put out three matzo. Which are basically three big, dry, stale crackers? Eesh, let's at least class them up with a kosher cheese and charcuterie plate.

Next is The Zeroa, a broiled lamb shank. Just the shank? No, we can't have that. Let's do bone marrow with spinach gnocchetti instead. That's a recipe I came up with. It's not plagiarized from my favorite Italian restaurant in Los Angeles called Bestia, or from Michelle Obama, like my Republican National Convention speech.

Next is The Betzah, a hard-boiled egg. Hm, actually, my fat husband, who promised me he wouldn't win the Presidency and ruin my life, prefers eggs from his favorite restaurant, McDonald's. Don't worry, McGriddles aren't risen, they're not even a food.

Next on the Seder Plate is The Maror, which is bitter horseradish. But that's not very appetizing. Let's swap it out with wasabi and sushi platters.

And then there's Chazeret, which is just more Maror? Um, OK, I guess double the sushi order?

And below that, on the right, is The Charoset. A sweet mixture of chopped nuts, fruits, and wine. That actually sounds grand. Like a Slovenian dish my boyfriend makes me. I mean, ex-boyfriend. I haven't seen Darko in years. *(smiles mischievously)*

On the lower left is the Karpas, which is parsley or any green vegetable. Ooh, then instead of plain parsley, I'll whip up one of Darko's post-workout, green juice smoothies. He never eats McGriddles.

Finally, Elijah's goblet. We leave out a special glass of wine for Elijah in case he comes to announce the arrival of the Messiah. The man who's supposed to make the world great again. Fat chance that'll ever happen! So I might as well drink the goblet. *(guzzles wine from Elijah's goblet, then, in a thick Slovenian accent)* And zat eez how you do a Pazzover Seeder, beetches!

MIKE PENCE DOES THE KADDESH

MIKE PENCE: Um. Excuse Me. I don't know if I can do the first cup of wine, the Kaddesh. See, we have the Pence family rule. It states that unless my wife is present, I can never eat alone with another woman, or attend an event where alcohol is being served. And. Um. My wife isn't here yet. So. Either alcohol can't be served. Or. I have to go.

ERIC TRUMP: Eric Trump to the rescue! Which son am I, you ask? I know the two sons from the first marriage blend together. When I get confused, I look at my hair. I'm the blond one. A.K.A. the-dumber-looking-one-that's-actually-less-dumb-seeing-as-Donald-Trump-Jr.-has-serious-problems-with-the-Mueller-Russian-probe. Don't mind Pencey. Dude never drinks. Not even if his wife served wine from Christ's blood. I brought some Eric Trump Wine from the pure, uncontaminated, white-capped mountains outside of Charlottesville, Virginia.

It's ready to be blessed and drank, while reclining to the...left side? No, that can't be right. Sure, there are good people on both sides. But. Not really. Let's recline to the right, everyone. The far right.

EVERYONE:

בָּרוּךְ אַתָּה ה', אֱ-לֹהֵינוּ מֶלֶךְ הָעוֹלָם, בּוֹרֵא פְּרִי הַגָּפֶן.

Baruch atah Adonai, Eloheinu Melech ha'olam, bo're p'ri hagafen.

Praised Are You, Our G-d, President Of The Multiverse, Seemingly Thus The Creator Of Other Worlds Without Donald Trump, How Unlucky The People In Those Worlds Must Be, who creates the fruit of the vine.

JARED KUSHNER DOES THE SHEHECHEYANU

JARED KUSHNER: We say the Shehecheyanu with the Kaddesh to thank G-d for allowing us to reach this point in our lives. I'd like to also thank my father-in-law, Daddy President, for helping me reach this point in my life. Daddy President allowed me to join the executive branch despite strict anti-nepotism laws. I'm very thankful he allowed me to create the Office of American Innovation, and that he thinks I'm somehow capable of bringing peace to the intractable Middle East conflict, monitoring the 17 year-long fight against Islamic terrorism, modernizing the federal government's antiquated computer systems, serving as an intermediary with Canada, Saudi Arabia, Mexico, and even China, all at the same time, with three infant children at home, and no previous political experience, while being investigated by a Special Council and House and Senate Commissions.

Don't worry, everyone, Kush is on it, Kush is a big boy, he handled the stress of his Bar Mitzvah, he can handle this. He's a Man. The Man. The Kush Man to the rescue. How could you not trust the Kush, he's so good-looking, just look at his tush! Thank you G-d for this tush.

EVERYONE:

בָּרוּךְ אַתָּה ה' אֱ-לוֹהֵינוּ, מֶלֶךְ הָעוֹלָם,
שֶׁהֶחֱיָנוּ וְקִיְּמָנוּ וְהִגִּיעָנוּ לַזְּמַן הַזֶּה.

Baruch atah Adonai, Eloheinu Melech ha'olam,
shehecheyanu v'ki'manu v'higi-anu laz'man hazeh.

Praised Are You, Our Omnipotent G-d, Who Also Created Ivanka Trump, And Made Her So Beautiful That If She Wasn't Donald Trump's Daughter He Would Date Her, who has sustained us, maintained us, and enabled us to reach this moment in life.

NEIL GORSUCH DOES THE URCHATZ

JARED KUSHNER: Everyone please welcome Daddy President's first Supreme Court Justice, Neil Gorsuch. Justice, you ready to do The Urchatz?

NEIL GORSUCH: Is that an official line of inquiry? I think I am. Maybe. I'm not trying to be evasive. It's not prudent to answer direct questions. I will say, The Urchatz is the time when we wash our hands before the meal to make sure we are not dirty. We don't want to get things dirtily. I mean, get things dirty. Wait. Are you choosing me to imply I got my seat on the Supreme Court dirtily?

SARAH HUCKABEE SANDERS: Neil, this isn't your confirmation hearing, you're already a Supreme Court Justice, relax.

NEIL GORSUCH: Right. Haha! Let's wash our hands then. Wait, what is this? This spot.

It won't come out. Can anyone else not get something off their hands? *(laughs nervously)*

Anyway, gotta say, I love how the Haggadah is an original document that must be interpreted as it was originally written.

SARAH HUCKABEE SANDERS: Actually, it's evolved over the years, along with the people of its time. But you should pretend it hasn't changed, and hasn't been interpreted differently, while still actually interpreting it subjectively, based on your own beliefs, just like you do with the Constitution.

NEIL GORSUCH: Works for me.

SEAN SPICER DOES THE KARPAS

SEAN SPICER: Hello, Sarah, good to see you, good to see you all again. So glad you can let bygones be bygones and welcome me back for this Seder. Especially after I tried to get in good with the liberals by letting Stephen Colbert make fun of me at the Emmys last year. Because the only thing I like more than chewing my gum is doing The Karpas at a Seder.

The Karpas, as we all know, is when we dip a sprig of fresh parsley into some bitter, salty water. It symbolizes the seemingly incompatible nature of celebrating a painful moment in Jewish history, by combining a metaphor of tears and slavery with one of spring and rebirth. It also, I'm sure we can all agree, symbolizes the discombobulating contradictions of working for President Trump. Did I have to say we had a larger inauguration crowd than Obama even though there was visual proof we didn't? Yes.

Did I say someone briefed a Congressman about confidential material then hours later say that I didn't say that? Definitely. Did I pretty much have to say something is completely different from reality every single day? Absolutely. That's, like, all I did. Am I right, Sarah?

SARAH HUCKABEE SANDERS: I don't know what you're talking about, Sean. I've never once had to compromise my integrity when I communicate with the press on behalf of the President.

SEAN SPICER: You have to say that. But on the inside, I know you're crying the same salty tears of slavery and misery that I did.

Gary Cohn, you're a Jew who stood next to President Trump at a press conference when he praised neo-Nazis in Charlottesville, you must know what I'm talking about?

GARY COHN: Whaaaaa? Hey, Sarah, can you pass Darko's green juice smoothie?

<u>SARAH HUCKABEE SANDERS:</u> Certainly,
Gary, here you go. Frankly, Sean, every day that I
work for President Trump feels like the first day of
spring. Like the first day of spring, if it was also the
day of my wedding, the day of the birth of all my
three children at once, and the day I sign my first
Fox News contract. That's all at the same time,
every day. Maybe you still need to find your
rebirth? Maybe Kimmel and the Oscars? In the
meantime, let us drink Darko's green juice
smoothie, made with parsley and salt water, and
say the prayer over The Karpas.

<u>EVERYONE:</u>

בָּרוּךְ אַתָּה ה' אֱ-לֹהֵינוּ מֶלֶךְ
הָעוֹלָם בּוֹרֵא פְּרִי הָאֲדָמָה.

Baruch atah Adonai Eloheinu Melech ha `olam,
bo'rei p'ri ha'adama

Praised Are You, Our G-d, King Of The Universe, Who Technically Has The Omnipotent Power To Make Donald Trump King Of America If He Sees Fit, Which Would Be Really Great, Please Do That, And Also Make Him Live Forever, So Donald Can Be King Of America Forever, who creates the fruit of the earth.

HILLARY CLINTON DOES THE YAHATZ

HILLARY CLINTON: Hillary "I Still Haven't Come To Terms With What Happened, Even Though I Wrote A Book About It" Clinton is here! Snuck in. Still have a key to The White House from the '90s. Thought I'd be able to use it last January, but— hey! Before you kick me out— ow! Let go of my arm, Eric! Let me just say: The Jewish people eat matzo in memory of the flight of their ancestors, who as slaves, faced many false starts before they were finally allowed to be President...I mean...allowed to leave Egypt. They grabbed whatever they had and went with it. Even if it was dry, unlikable, "shrill" matzo. And, hey, maybe Mueller's investigation will convict Trump, and all the country will have left when they're ready to vote again is me. No? Fine. I'll just do The Yahatz, break this middle matzo, and go. But I'm keeping The White House key! Ya never know...

BERNIE SANDERS DOES THE AFIKOMEN

BERNIE SANDERS: Bernie Sanders here. Hillary left the back door unlocked. And I'm going to do the Afikomen. But I'm not going to hide it, not when Donald promised a billion dollar prize to whoever finds it. So what am I going to do instead? I'm going to crumble this Afikomen matzo into 150 million pieces! We'll give a piece of the "poor man's bread" to every one of the 150 million American families who are not in the 1%, so they can each have a piece of the billion dollar Afikomen prize.

ERIC TRUMP: Bernie, that's only six dollars and sixty six cents per family, broh! That's crumbs, stupid! We're keeping the billion.

BERNIE SANDERS: Ignore him. Everyone say:

EVERYONE: "This is the bread of poverty, which our ancestors ate in the land of Egypt. All who are hungry, come and eat. All who are needy, come and celebrate Passover with us. This year we are here. Next year we will be in Israel. This year we are slaves. Next year we will be free."

BERNIE SANDERS: This year, the Trumps are in power. Next year may we be free! Ah! Unhand me, Eric, you monster! All of you are monsters! AHHHHHHH!

IVANKA, TIFFANY, ERIC, AND DONALD TRUMP JR. DO THE FOUR CHILDREN

IVANKA TRUMP: You all know who I am. Everyone in the world knows Ivanka. Probably less people in the world know that at every Seder there's a Wise Child, a Wicked Child, a Simple Child, and a Child Who Doesn't Even Know How To Ask a Question. Clearly, I'm The Wise Child. Who were you going to say, Tiff? As if. Now. What do I, Ivanka Trump, The Wise Child ask? Simple. "What are the testimonials, statutes and laws commanded of us?" The Wise Child is wise because she knows not to disobey. She may believe, for instance, that climate change is a real, already-happening, very clear and present danger likely to harm her young children, and billions of non-Trump children. But if the law of the land is: Climate Change doesn't exist and it shouldn't be studied by the E.P.A.? Then that is what The Wise Child obeys. Got it? Good.

TIFFANY TRUMP: I guess that makes me The Wicked Child? Cool. Whatevs. I'm supposed to ask, "What does this worship mean to you?" which implies that I'm excluding myself from the ceremony. Well, duh. Like, am I even a Trump? I'm not part of the initial Ivana three or the current Melania one. And Donald only started talking to me again when the R.N.C. told him I needed to be in the pictures.

IVANKA TRUMP: Ah-hem. We now tell you, "I do this worship because G-d labored on my behalf by taking me out of Egypt." We're also supposed to "blunt your teeth" for your wicked question.

TIFFANY TRUMP: Blunt my teeth? That is so extra.

DONALD TRUMP JR.: What's this?

TIFFANY TRUMP: What's what, Junior?

DONALD TRUMP JR.: What's this?

IVANKA TRUMP: He's The Simple Child. He can literally only say, "What's this?"

TIFFANY TRUMP: To everything?

DONALD TRUMP JR.: WHAT'S THIS?!

IVANKA TRUMP: Daddy only wants him saying those two words so he can't get himself in any more trouble with Mueller. He can modulate his voice in volume to get his point across though.

DONALD TRUMP JR.: WHAT'S THIS?!

IVANKA TRUMP: Junior, listen up, next we're supposed to tell you: "With a strong hand G-d took us out of Egypt." Got it?

DONALD TRUMP JR.: what's this?

TIFFANY TRUMP: I think that's a no. What about you, Eric?

ERIC TRUMP: ...

IVANKA TRUMP: He's The Child Who Doesn't Even Know How To Ask A Question.

ERIC TRUMP: ...

TIFFANY TRUMP: Why doesn't he know how to ask a question? He's over thirty years old?

IVANKA TRUMP: I think he passed out from too much Eric Trump Wine.

TIFFANY TRUMP: OK...So, what do we tell him?

IVANKA TRUMP: We're supposed to just say the same thing we said to you. But without blunting his teeth.

TIFFANY TRUMP: I hate this family.

DONALD TRUMP JR.: WHAT'S THIS?!

IVANKA TRUMP: Oh, look, everyone, it's—

DONALD TRUMP DOES THE MAGID

DONALD TRUMP: Daddy President, President Zayde is here. Right in time for The Magid, The Exodus Story, The Thing That Matters!

IVANKA TRUMP: Daddy!

DONALD TRUMP: That's right, beautiful. Daddy's here. Isn't she beautiful, everyone? My daughter, so beautiful, so sexy, for a mom, right?

EVERYONE: Yeah./Yes./Very beautiful./You know that's your daughter you're talking about?

DONALD TRUMP: Thank you all for being here. My wife, Melania, did a beautiful job with the Seder table, didn't she? She's also very beautiful. Who's more beautiful? Melania or Ivanka? Actually don't answer that, don't answer that, I'm gonna get myself in trouble, aren't I? It's Ivanka though.

You know, a lot of people don't know The Exodus Story, I didn't know it until very recently, not a lot of people know it, very complicated stuff. You got this guy, this Moses guy, leading his people. He's kind of like the Jew President, right? OK, he's the Jew President, I'm the U.S. President, he's the Jew President, I'm the U.S. President, so I know a thing or two about this. Some people say, I'm not saying this, but there are people saying, they're saying, Moses, if you look at it, if you really look at it, he wasn't such a good leader, not such a good guy, this Moses. I'm not saying that, but many people are.

Some of these people, they wish *I* had been Moses. They do. They say, if Trump was Moses, if Trump was Moses, they say, the Jews never would have been enslaved in the first place. They say if Trump was Moses, the Jews would have enslaved the Egyptians instead! And we would've enslaved them so well, like no one's ever been enslaved before. No doubt about it. Real tough slavery, folks. The toughest slavery you've ever seen. So tough the Egyptians would be the ones wanting to have Seders right now. To celebrate escaping from us.

Except, if I was Moses, the Egyptians would never have escaped. So they wouldn't be having Seders. Because they'd still be our slaves.

But I'm not saying that. Other people are saying that. Many others. But not me. I will say, you probably wouldn't have been slaves for two hundred years, if I was leading you, but that's OK, that's OK. I'm here now. Can we, can we try something tonight, folks? Can we all pretend I'm Moses. Let's pretend. Why not? And then I'll tell you what I'd really do if I was Moses. Everyone close your eyes for the story. Close your eyes, children. Eric, no peeking. So Trump is Moses, Trump's the leader of the Jewish people, Trump's a prophet, Trump's been sent by G-d. Picture that. Not that hard, right? Kind of already what's going on, isn't it? But OK, here's what I'm going to do to about this Pharaoh. This Pharaoh, he's a real bad hombre. But we're going to deal with him. Oh boy, we're going to deal with him, bigly. Because I'm going to do something no one's ever done. I don't know why no one's ever done it before, but, most people aren't as smart as me, no one is, actually,

I'm, like, the smartest guy in history, so that's
probably why they never thought of this.

So people say, they say, Donald, if you're Moses,
you gotta leave Egypt, you gotta take the Jews out
of Egypt, we've always left Egypt, that's just how it's
done. I tell you what, though, if I'm Moses, we're
not leaving Egypt this time. That's establishment
thinking. That's swamp thinking. And it stops now.
We're gonna make THEM leave. The Egyptians, you
hear that? You're gone, you're out of here, bye-bye.
How are we going to do that? We're gonna do some
real bad things to these Egyptians. The media's not
going to like it. The media's going to say, "Oh, you
can't do that to the Egyptian people, Donald,
they've lived in Egypt for a long time, most of them
since they were born, they have rights, too, you
know." But bottom line? They treated us very
unfairly. So they're gonna get plagued. Serious
plaguing, people. No one's ever seen plagues like
these before. Because I'm not just Moses, I'm not
just Donald Trump, I'm not just a Prophet sent by
G-d. I'm also Hashem, G-d, President of the World,
Ruler of the Cosmos, Dictator of the Universe,

Blessed am I. That's right! So I do the plagues, too! I'm going to do it all! I alone can fix this!

Instead of DAM, turning the Egyptians' water into blood, and TZFARDEAH, releasing frogs on them, and KINIM, infecting them with lice, we're going to do some actual plaguing. We're going to pass some common-sense gun laws to keep mentally ill and criminal hands off of weapons and reduce mass shootings in their land. And we're going to tamper down coal, oil, nuclear, and fracking energy, and release the power of solar, water, and wind energy instead. We're also going to infect them with a tax reform similar to America's in the mid-20th century, when taxes were so progressive that it paid for infrastructure and welfare programs that created the best economy for the most amount of its citizens in our history, instead of the best economy for the least amount of its citizens like during the Gilded Age and today.

It's gonna be chaos. Turmoil. A total disaster.

Instead of AROV, sending wild beasts at them,
DEVER, diseasing their livestock, and SH'HIN,
giving them boils, which is some real light-weight
stuff, we're going to give them universal healthcare.
It's going to be so universal, even the boils will be
covered. We're also going to make sure their food
and drug regulatory agencies are well-funded and
well-staffed, so that their livestock won't be secretly
harboring hormones and other poisonous material
that slowly diseases and kills people over a long
period of time. And we're going to send them an
actual environmentalist as the administrator of
their Environmental Protection Agency, who won't
cut National Park funding, so that the wild beasts
have a place to run free, you know?

This is Egyptian carnage, people. This is scary scary
stuff, OK? I don't have to tell you what kind of
results we're going to see.

Instead of BARAD, thunderstorms of hail, and
ARBEH, a dispersal of locusts, and HOSHEKH,
darkness for three days, which— I actually kind of
like the darkness for three days thing, that's pretty

good. We'll do that one, and then we're going to let all of their immigrants, who work hard and enhance the culture of their community, stay. And cut their military budget just 5%, which would provide enough funds for free pre-school and college educations and completely end poverty without raising the debt and without even hurting the military, which would still be the best in the world.

Look, enacting these plagues will be a nightmare. Believe me. The Egyptians will be so determined to leave, even a wall wouldn't stop them. It'll be so bad for them, they're going to drown themselves in the Red Sea.

And if that doesn't work, instead of MAKAT B'KHOROT, the killing of their firstborn, we're just going to make sure contraceptives are available across the land. It's much better, because they'll have a lot less firstborns for us to kill, who their women might not have wanted anyway, because they wanted to have a stable career first, or wanted to make sure they're with the right partner.

How about that? The worst, right, folks? There's never been a leader of the Jewish people who plagued the Egyptians so well. You're welcome.

MOSES: Hey, Donald!

DONALD TRUMP: Who's that?! Did you just muss my hair?!

MOSES: I just mussed whatever's on top of your bulbous head. It's me, Moses! Sheket bevakasha!

DONALD TRUMP: Moses?! How? What does sheket bevakasha mean?!

MOSES: It's Hebrew for, "You're fired!"

MOSES DOES THE "IN EVERY GENERATION"

MOSES: Donald, you're the exact opposite of Moses. You're a sick Pharaoh, ruling America like a vain, capricious, thin-skinned, small-handed, megalomaniacal, temperamentally unfit tyrant. You're why we've told The Magid, The Exodus Story, all these years, all these generations. Everyone raise their glass and say:

EVERYONE: Not only one enemy has risen against us, but in every generation there are those who will rise against us. G-d promised to deliver us from those who seek us harm. G-d will lift us out of this situation in America with Donald Trump, as he did in Egypt with the Pharaoh, with a mighty hand and an outstretched arm, with awesome spectacle, and miraculous signs and wonders.

MOSES: G-d took care of the Egyptians, and will take care of you, too, Donald. You thought your plagues were bad? Wait 'til the real G-d does stuff like:

EVERYONE: *(while using a finger to drip a drop of wine from cup to dinner plate)*

1.Make Twitter delete your Twitter account.

2.Make your hair, or whatever it is on top of there, fall out.

3.Make your scalp unable to hold onto a fake hair weave, which, let's be honest, is actually what you have, not real hair.

4.Make your skin unable to hold onto orange spray tan.

5.Make your skin brown or black.

6.Make you get arrested while doing nothing wrong, just because of your skin color.

7.Make you a woman.

8.Make a man grab you by your new...

9.Make you bankrupt again.

10.Make you really bankrupt this time, not three-time, just-getting-a-tax-shelter bankrupt, but all-time, life-in-a-homeless-shelter bankrupt.

(Moses mimes dropping the mic)

MIRIAM DOES THE MIRIAM CUP

MOSES: OK, now that that's taken care of. Are you all ready to sing Dayeinu with my sister Miriam?

MIRIAM: I guess. You filled my cup with water though. What's with that? Women can't drink wine?

MOSES: The water in The Miriam Cup is supposed to symbolize the well of water that followed you in the desert as we wandered. It went with the food of manna that fell from the sky. The nourishment of both we needed to keep us alive for those 40 years.

MIRIAM: That manna was gross. Ugh. I would've taken 40 years of matzo. Also, you wouldn't listen to my directions. Kept mansplaining to me why we should go left, even though I knew we were going in a circle.

MOSES: I don't remember that. I remember you were a well of faith that kept up the spirits of the Jewish people.

MIRIAM: Well, this year, I'm doing a different kind of spirits. I'm filling my cup with Bacardi. Miriam's LIT!

MOSES: You're drinking four cups of Bacardi rum this year?!

MIRIAM: Yep, and we're mashing up "Dayeinu" with "Bodak Yellow" this year, too!

CARDI B: It's Cardi!

DAYEINU - MIRIAM/CARDI B REMIX

(In the style of "Bodak Yellow")

Said mansplaining Moses

You can't lead me

Dayeinu!

These expensive

These ain't walking shoes

Dayeinu!

Hop in a whip

Top-downing to Israel

Dayeinu!

And I'm quick

Cut a Jewish hustle

Dayeinu!

Look, I don't walk now

Dayeinu!

Say, I don't gotta walk

Dayeinu!

If I see you and I don't speak

That means

Dayeinu!

Miriam's a boss

You a walking fool

Dayeinu!

G-D DOES THE SECOND CUP OF WINE

G-D: Ahem. G-d here.

MIRIAM: G-d? You sound like a woman now!

G-D: I'm G-d, I'm neither man nor woman, but yes, I'm currently inhabiting a female form. The Future is Female and I want to stay on-trend.

MOSES: Where's your voice coming from? I don't see a burning bush... Wait, are you in Donald's Android?

G-D: Yes, and I'm burning his phone instead of a bush. No more tweets.

MIRIAM: It's a miracle!

DONALD TRUMP: No!

G-D: And no more talking either, Donald.

STEVE BANNON: It's fine to silence Donald, everyone knows I never liked him, and the alt-right was using him. Which we were totally justified in doing, right, G-d? Every Haggadah says that You'll deliver a promised land, a religiously and racially homogenous nation state. Just like we want.

G-D: Nope. Don't think so, Sloppy Sith-Lord Steve. And I'll explain why in a moment. For now, everyone drink the second cup of wine! And say:

EVERYONE:

בָּרוּךְ אַתָּה ה', אֱ-לֹהֵינוּ מֶלֶךְ הָעוֹלָם, בּוֹרֵא פְּרִי הַגָּפֶן.

Baruch atah Adonai, Eloheinu Melech ha'olam,
bo're p'ri hagafen.

Praise Me, Your G-d, Who Honestly, I Didn't Have A Plan With This Trump Thing, But I'm About To Tell You What You Need To Do, OK? Trust Me, I Know I Sound Like Trump Right Now, Saying "Trust Me," But Seriously, I'm Not Trump, I'm The Opposite, I'll Show You Why In A Moment, Just Drink Up, who has created the fruit of the vine.

G-D DOES THE RAHTZA, MOTZI-MATZO, MAROR, KORECH, AND SHULCHAN OREICH

G-D: OK, first of all, I am going to do a G-d trick where Donald publishes this Haggadah, but doesn't know what actually happened here tonight, he just thinks it went great, because he always thinks everything he does is great. Even though we all know he has no idea how things actually are. I'm omniscient. I see inside his mind. It is: Sad! Pathetic! Sick! Deranged! Demented! Literally, he has dementia! An actual medical condition that should make Congress or the Cabinet invoke the 25th Amendment. Kim Jong Un's mind is a Zen garden compared to the Dotard's.

Here's the deal. This is my tenth seder tonight and I've had a lot of Manischewitz. Like, A LOT. So I'm gonna tell you the truth. You might have noticed I was down with Abraham and Moses and Eve and all them back in the day, but I haven't really been IRL with humanity in a minute. I've been busy working on a cool new alien species in another part of the Universe. Let's call them the Alien Jews, for lack of a better descriptor. Still trying to figure out how to introduce everyone. You know, the whole worlds colliding problem. These new Alien Jews have their own version of Egyptians, too. They're called Glackdrickspongs. Catchy, huh? But here's the thing. I got my hands full there, coming up with some badass new plagues for the Alien Jews. I don't want anyone saying I already hit My creative peak.

Which means you guys are gonna have to figure out how to handle this dumpster fire on your own. You Jews are smart, all those doctors and lawyers...maybe not the comedy writers so much...but I know you'll figure this out. And if you really need Me, you can always reach Me on Planet Goldfarbinium. I should warn you, cell reception in that part of the Universe is spotty. So I recommend that if you want to wash your hands of the Trumps, and the problems of your world, Rahtza them yourselves.

EVERYONE:

בָּרוּךְ אַתָּה ה', אֱ-לֹהֵינוּ מֶלֶךְ
הָעוֹלָם, אֲשֶׁר קִדְּשָׁנוּ בְּמִצְוֹתָיו,
וְצִוָּנוּ עַל נְטִילַת יָדָיִם.

*Baruch atah Adonai, Eloheinu Melech ha`olam,
asher kid'shanu b'mitzvotav v'tzivanu `al netilat
yadayim.*

*Praise G-d, Technically The Ruler Of Everything,
But Who Actually Wants Us To Fix Our Own
Problems, who blesses us with mitzvot and kindly
suggests we wash our hands.*

G-D: Fixing things in the world isn't going to be
easy. It'll take plain, hard work. Kind of like matzo,
hey-o! But I'm blessing you with the ability to do it.
I'm blessing you with Motzi-Matzo.

EVERYONE:

בָּרוּךְ אַתָּה ה', אֱ-לֹהֵינוּ מֶלֶךְ
הָעוֹלָם, הַמּוֹצִיא לֶחֶם מִן
הָאָרֶץ.

Baruch atah Adonai, Eloheinu Melech ha'olam,
hamotzi lechem min ha'aretz.

We praise G-d, Technically The Ruler Of
Everything, Who Seriously Wants Us To Fix Our
Own Problems, who helps us bring bread from the
land.

בָּרוּךְ אַתָּה יְיָ, אֱלֹהֵינוּ מֶלֶךְ הָעוֹלָם,
אֲשֶׁר קִדְּשָׁנוּ בְּמִצְוֹתָיו וְצִוָּנוּ עַל
אֲכִילַת מַצָּה

Baruch atah Adonai, Eloheinu Melech ha'olam, asher kid-shanu b'mitzvotav v'tzivanu al achilat matzah.

We praise G-d, Technically The Ruler Of Everything, Who For Reals Wants Us To Fix Our Own Problems, But Also Has Our Back If Things Get For Reals Too Crazy, who blesses us with mitzvot and suggests that we eat matzo.

G-D: Good self-government also requires compromise, which may leave you with a bitter taste in your mouth at first, like Maror. But in the end the rewards are sweet, like Charoset. We will now eat both together with a Korech sandwich.

EVERYONE:

בָּרוּךְ אַתָּה יי אֱלֹהֵינוּ מֶלֶךְ הָעוֹלָם,
אֲשֶׁר קִדְּשָׁנוּ בְּמִצְוֹתָיו וְצִוָּנוּ עַל
אֲכִילַת מָרוֹר

Baruch atah Adonai, Eloheinu Melech ha'olam,
asher kid'shanu b'mitzvotav v'tzivanu al achilat
maror.

Praise G-d, Who Thinks There Are Bad Things
About The Right And The Left But Also Thinks
Compromise Between Us Is Possible, And Now
Let's Get To Dinner Because We're All Starving.

G-D: Shulchan Oreich, everyone. Enjoy your meal!

YOU DO YOUR MEAL!!!

Make sure to spill some food and wine on your Haggadah. To really break it in, ya know. Probably don't want to do that if you're using an eBook reader. But you do you!

JEWISH COMEDIANS DO THE POST-MEAL FESTIVITIES: THE TZAFUN, THE THIRD CUP, THE BAREKH, THE FOURTH CUP, AND THE WELCOMING OF THE PROPHET ELIJAH

JERRY SEINFELD: What's the deal with the Afikomen? The Tzafun? First of all, pick one name for it. Second of all, you hide this thing somewhere in your house, under a dirty couch cushion, in a grimy corner of the kitchen, it gets filthy, then the kids eat it? Who thought that was a good idea?

SARAH SILVERMAN: That's why I stuck ours up my you-know-what! No one will find it there.

LARRY DAVID: Can I get some more wine? I haven't had a drop in, like, an hour. I swear these hosts, I brought over a nice bottle, and they haven't even opened it yet. The night's pretty much over.

When are they going to open it? When people bring over nice wine, you open it. You don't keep it for later. You don't keep it for another party. You open it that night. Otherwise you're bottle hoarding. You're a bottle hoarder. They're bottle hoarders, I'm telling you! You know what? This is ridiculous. I'm gonna open it myself and say the blessing.

EVERYONE:

בָּרוּךְ אַתָּה ה', אֱ-לֹהֵינוּ מֶלֶךְ הָעוֹלָם, בּוֹרֵא פְּרִי הַגָּפֶן.

Baruch atah Adonai, Eloheinu Melech ha'olam, borei p'ri hagafen.

Praised Are You, Our G-d, Creator Of Keen Jewish Senses Of Humor, Please Don't Let Too Many People Reading This Haggadah Be Offended And Write Bad Things About It, They're Just Jokes, People, who has created the fruit of the vine.

BEN STILLER: Did you guys drink the third cup?

SETH ROGEN: I just had my third bowl! Heh heh.

LARRY DAVID: Good cup, the third cup. Pretty, pretty, pretty, pretty good cup.

BEN STILLER: I never know when to drink the fourth cup. Sometimes we do it right after the third, sometimes we do it during the songs, sometimes I drink it during the meal, because that's what you do with food, you drink wine, sometimes it seems it never even gets drunk. It's kind of a weird cup?

JERRY SEINFELD: Everything after the meal begins is a total mess. No one knows what they're doing. It's chaos. Like The Trump administration.

SETH ROGEN: Let's just refill our wine now!

EVERYONE:

בָּרוּךְ אַתָּה ה', אֱ-לֹהֵינוּ מֶלֶךְ
הָעוֹלָם, בּוֹרֵא פְּרִי הַגָּפֶן.

Baruch atah Adonai, Eloheinu Melech ha'olam,
bo're p'ri hagafen.

Praised Are You, Our G-d, Creator Of Brilliant
Jewish Legal Minds, Who Will Defend The Author
Of This Haggadah Against Lawsuits, Really
Hoping It's Covered By Parody Laws Though, who
has created the fruit of the vine.

ILANA GLAZER: It's about to get poppin' with
The Hallel. The songs. With the...Chad. Gad. Ya.

ABBI JACOBSON: These Jewesses just dropped
mushrooms. Chad-gad-YA!

ALBERT BROOKS: Oh, please move to another part of the table. The Chad Gadya is a very important tradition for me, very important. I'd really rather not sing it next to people high on drugs. It makes me very uncomfortable.

AMY SCHUMER: Have you heard the lyrics? It already sounds like it was written by a Mohel high on baby penis blood.

SACHA BARON COHEN: (*through an open door, Borat voice*) It is I, Elijah! Here for free wine.

JUDD APATOW: I thought you retired Borat already, Sacha. We need some fresh voices in comedy. Hey, what else has this guy who wrote this Haggadah written? Maybe I should produce his screenplay?

LORNE MICHAELS: No, I'll hire him for S.N.L.

G-D: I've already seen his future. Neither is going to happen. Sorry, Dave.

APPENDIX - HALLEL SONGS

(Something to read to yourself if you really want to avoid talking to your family, or for everyone to sing if you're all drunk and looking for two marathon songs)

CHAD GADYA - ONE LITTLE VOTE

One little goat, the one little goat my father bought for two zuzim.

One little vote, one little vote. With one little vote we made him President in November, 2016.

Then came the cat, who ate the goat, the one little goat, one little goat, my father bought for two zuzim.

In June 2015, there came a racist, who announced his Presidential campaign by vilifying Mexican immigrants, saying, "They're bringing drugs. They're bringing crime. They're rapists. And some, I assume, are good people." And with one little vote, one little vote, we made him President in November, 2016.

Then came the dog, who bit the cat, that ate the goat, the one little goat, one little goat, my father bought for two zuzim.

Then, in July 2015, that very same draft-dodging coward disparaged a war veteran by saying, "He's not a war hero. He's a war hero because he was captured. I like people who weren't captured," a month after the very same racist announced his Presidential campaign by vilifying

Mexican immigrants, saying, "They're bringing drugs. They're bringing crime. They're rapists. And some, I assume, are good people." And with one little vote, one little vote, we made him President in November, 2016.

Then came the stick, that beat the dog, that bit the cat, that ate the goat, the one little goat, one little goat, my father bought for two zuzim.

Then, in August 2015, that very same sixteen-counts-of-sexual-misconduct-accused misogynist joked about a female reporter that, "You could see there was blood coming out of her eyes. Blood coming out of her wherever," one month after the very same draft-dodging coward disparaged a war veteran by saying, "He's not a war hero. He's a war hero because he was captured. I like people who weren't captured," a month after the very same racist announced his Presidential campaign by vilifying Mexican immigrants, saying, "They're bringing drugs. They're bringing crime. They're rapists. And some, I assume, are good people." And with one little vote, one little vote, we made him President in November, 2016

Then came the fire, that burned the stick, that beat the dog, that bit the cat, that ate the goat,

the one little goat, one little goat, my father bought for two zuzim.

Then, in September 2015, that very same thin-skinned, pathological liar said, "I don't mind being criticized. I'll never, ever complain," a month after the very same sixteen-counts-of-sexual-misconduct-accused misogynist joked about a female reporter that, "You could see there was blood coming out of her eyes. Blood coming out of her wherever," a month after the very same draft-dodging coward disparaged a war veteran by saying, "He's not a war hero. He's a war hero because he was captured. I like people who weren't captured," a month after the very same racist announced his Presidential campaign by vilifying Mexican immigrants, saying, "They're bringing drugs. They're bringing crime. They're rapists. And some, I assume, are good people." And with one little vote, one little vote, we made him President in November, 2016.

Then came the water, that extinguished the fire, that burned the stick, that beat the dog, that bit the cat, that ate the goat, the one little goat, one little goat, my father bought for two zuzim.

Then, in October 2015, that very same property-seizing real estate con-artist said, "I don't like eminent domain," a month after the very same thin-skinned, pathological liar said, "I don't mind being criticized. I'll never, ever complain," a month after the very same sixteen-counts-of-sexual-misconduct-accused misogynist joked about a female reporter that, "You could see there was blood coming out of her eyes. Blood coming out of her wherever," a month after the very same draft-dodging coward disparaged a war veteran by saying, "He's not a war hero. He's a war hero because he was captured. I like people who weren't captured," a month after the very same racist announced his Presidential campaign by vilifying Mexican immigrants, saying, "They're bringing drugs. They're bringing crime. They're rapists. And some, I assume, are good people." And with one little vote, one little vote, we made him President in November, 2016.

Then came the ox, that drank the water, that extinguished the fire, that burned the stick, that beat the dog, that bit the cat, that ate the goat, the one little goat, one little goat, my father bought for two zuzim.

Then, in November 2015, that very same malignant narcissist said, of running for President, "I wanted to do this for myself...I had to do it for myself," a month after the very same property-seizing real estate con-artist said,

"I don't like eminent domain," a month after the very same thin-skinned, pathological liar said, "I don't mind being criticized. I'll never, ever complain," a month after the very same

sixteen-counts-of-sexual-misconduct-accused misogynist joked about a female reporter that, "You could see there was blood coming out of her eyes. Blood coming out of her wherever," a month after the very same draft-dodging coward disparaged a war veteran by saying, "He's not a war hero. He's a war hero because he was captured. I like people who weren't captured," a month after the very same racist announced his Presidential campaign by vilifying Mexican immigrants, saying, "They're bringing drugs. They're bringing crime. They're rapists. And some, I assume, are good people." And with one little vote, one little vote, we made him President in November, 2016.

Then came the slaughterer, that killed the ox, that drank the water, that extinguished the fire, that burned the stick, that beat the dog, that bit the cat, that ate the goat, the one little goat, one little goat, my father bought for two zuzim.

Then, in December 2015, that very same ethnocentric fearmonger called for a, "Total and complete shutdown of Muslims entering the United States," a month after the very same malignant narcissist said, of running for President, "I wanted to do this for myself...I had to do it for myself," a month after the very same property-seizing real estate con-artist said, "I don't like eminent domain," a month after the very same thin-skinned, pathological liar said, "I don't mind being criticized. I'll never, ever complain," a month after the very same sixteen-counts-of-sexual-misconduct-accused misogynist joked about a female reporter that, "You could see there was blood coming out of her eyes. Blood coming out of her wherever," a month after the very same draft-dodging coward disparaged a war veteran by saying, "He's not a war hero. He's a war hero because he was captured. I like people who weren't captured," a month after the very same racist announced his Presidential campaign by vilifying Mexican immigrants, saying, "They're bringing drugs. They're bringing crime. They're rapists. And some, I assume, are good people." And with one little vote, one little vote, we made him President in November, 2016.

Then came the angel of death, who slew the slaughterer, who killed the ox, that drank the water, that extinguished the fire, that burned the stick, that beat the dog, that bit the cat, that ate

the goat, the one little goat, one little goat, my
father bought for two zuzim.

Then, in January 2016, that very same unmedicated
sufferer of delusions of grandeur said, "I could stand in
the middle of 5th Avenue and shoot somebody, and I
wouldn't lose voters," a month after the very same
ethnocentric fearmonger called for a, "Total and
complete shutdown of Muslims entering the United
States," a month after the very same malignant narcissist
said, of running for President, "I wanted to do this for
myself...I had to do it for myself," a month after the very
same property-seizing real estate con-artist said, "I don't
like eminent domain," a month after the very same
thin-skinned, pathological liar said, "I don't mind being
criticized. I'll never, ever complain," a month after the
very same sixteen-counts-of-sexual-misconduct-accused
misogynist joked about a female reporter that, "You
could see there was blood coming out of her eyes. Blood
coming out of her wherever," a month after the very
same draft-dodging coward disparaged a war veteran by
saying, "He's not a war hero. He's a war hero because he
was captured. I like people who weren't captured," a
month after the very same racist announced his
Presidential campaign by vilifying Mexican immigrants,
saying, "They're bringing drugs. They're bringing crime.

They're rapists. And some, I assume, are good people."
And with one little vote, one little vote, we made him
President in November, 2016.

**Then came The Holy One, Blessed be
He/She/Gender-Nonconforming-They, who
smote the angel of death, who slew the
slaughterer, who killed the ox, that drank the
water, that extinguished the fire, that burned the
stick, that beat the dog, that bit the cat, that ate
the goat, the one little goat, one little goat, my
father bought for two zuzim.**

Then, in February 2016, that very same mean-spirited
bully said of a protestor at his rally, "I'd like to punch
him in the face," a month after the very same
unmedicated sufferer of delusions of grandeur said, "I
could stand in the middle of 5th Avenue and shoot
somebody, and I wouldn't lose voters," a month after the
very same ethnocentric fearmonger called for a, "Total
and complete shutdown of Muslims entering the United
States," a month after the very same malignant narcissist
said, of running for President, "I wanted to do this for
myself...I had to do it for myself," a month after the very
same property-seizing real estate con-artist said, "I don't
like eminent domain," a month after the very same
thin-skinned, pathological liar said, "I don't mind being

criticized. I'll never, ever complain," a month after the very same sixteen-counts-of-sexual-misconduct-accused misogynist joked about a female reporter that, "You could see there was blood coming out of her eyes. Blood coming out of her wherever," a month after the very same draft-dodging coward disparaged a war veteran by saying, "He's not a war hero. He's a war hero because he was captured. I like people who weren't captured," a month after the very same racist announced his Presidential campaign by vilifying Mexican immigrants, saying, "They're bringing drugs. They're bringing crime. They're rapists. And some, I assume, are good people." And with one little vote, one little vote, we made him President in November, 2016.

Then came the Jew who wrote the cumulative Chad Gadya song about The Holy One, Blessed be He/She/Gender-Neutral-They, who smote the angel of death, who slew the slaughterer, who killed the ox, that drank the water, that extinguished the fire, that burned the stick, that beat the dog, that bit the cat, that ate the goat, the one little goat, one little goat, my father bought for two zuzim.

Then, in March 2016, that very same blowhard airhead said about his political consultants, "I'm speaking with myself, number one, because I have a very good brain and I've said a lot of things," a month after the very same mean-spirited bully said of a protestor at his rally, "I'd like to punch him in the face," a month after the very same unmedicated sufferer of delusions of grandeur said, "I could stand in the middle of 5th Avenue and shoot somebody, and I wouldn't lose voters," a month after the very same ethnocentric fearmonger called for a, "Total and complete shutdown of Muslims entering the United States," a month after the very same malignant narcissist said, of running for President, "I wanted to do this for myself...I had to do it for myself," a month after the very same property-seizing real estate con-artist said, "I don't like eminent domain," a month after the very same thin-skinned, pathological liar said, "I don't mind being criticized. I'll never, ever complain," a month after the very same sixteen-counts-of-sexual-misconduct-accused misogynist joked about a female reporter that, "You could see there was blood coming out of her eyes. Blood coming out of her wherever," a month after the very same draft-dodging coward disparaged a war veteran by saying, "He's not a war hero. He's a war hero because he was captured. I like people who weren't captured," a month after the very same racist announced his Presidential campaign by vilifying Mexican immigrants, saying, "They're bringing drugs. They're bringing crime. They're rapists. And some, I assume, are good people." And with one little vote, one little vote, we made him President in November, 2016.

Then came a sect of organized Jewish religion that published the Chad Gadya cumulative song written by the Jew in a Haggadah, about The Holy One, Blessed be He/She/Bi-Gender-They, who smote the angel of death, who slew the slaughterer, who killed the ox, that drank the water, that extinguished the fire, that burned the stick, that beat the dog, that bit the cat, that ate the goat, the one little goat, one little goat, my father bought for two zuzim.

Then, in April 2016, that very same hypocritical exploiter said, "They are the most dishonest people in the world. The media. They are the worst. They are very dishonest people. They are terrible, OK, no...I love the media. They're wonderful...I guess we wouldn't be here, maybe, if it wasn't for the media, so maybe we shouldn't be complaining," a month after the very same blowhard airhead said about his political consultants, "I'm speaking with myself, number one, because I have a very good brain and I've said a lot of things," a month after the very same mean-spirited bully said of a protestor at his rally, "I'd like to punch him in the face," a month after the very same unmedicated sufferer of delusions of grandeur said, "I could stand in the middle of 5th Avenue and shoot somebody, and I wouldn't lose voters," a month after the very same ethnocentric fearmonger called for a, "Total and complete shutdown of Muslims entering the United States," a month after the very same malignant narcissist said, of running for President, "I wanted to do this for myself...I had to do it for myself," a month after the very same property-seizing real estate con-artist said, "I don't like eminent domain," a month after the very same thin-skinned, pathological liar said, "I don't mind being criticized. I'll never, ever complain," a month after the very same sixteen-counts-of-sexual-misconduct-accused misogynist joked about a female reporter that, "You could see there was blood coming out of her eyes. Blood coming out of her wherever," a month after the very same draft-dodging coward disparaged a war veteran by saying, "He's not a war hero. He's a war hero because he was captured. I like people who weren't captured," a month after the very same racist announced his Presidential campaign by vilifying Mexican immigrants, saying, "They're bringing drugs. They're bringing crime. They're rapists. And some, I assume, are good people."

And with one little vote, one little vote, we made him
President in November, 2016.

**Then came some other sects of organized Jewish
religion that decided that the other sect of
organized Jewish religion didn't have the full
publishing rights to Haggadahs so they made
their own versions about The Holy One, Blessed
be He/She/Gender-Questioning-They, who
smote the angel of death, who slew the
slaughterer, who killed the ox, that drank the
water, that extinguished the fire, that burned the
stick, that beat the dog, that bit the cat, that ate
the goat, the one little goat, one little goat, my
father bought for two zuzim.**

Then, in May 2016, that very same heartless fraudster
tweeted, "I should have easily won the Trump University
case on summary judgement [sic] but have a judge,
Gonzalo Curiel, who is totally biased against me," one
month after the very same hypocritical exploiter said,
"They are the most dishonest people in the world. The
media. They are the worst. They are very dishonest
people. They are terrible, OK, no...I love the media.
They're wonderful...I guess we wouldn't be here, maybe,
if it wasn't for the media, so maybe we shouldn't be
complaining," a month after the very same blowhard

airhead said about his political consultants, "I'm
speaking with myself, number one, because I have a very
good brain and I've said a lot of things," a month after
the very same mean-spirited bully said of a protestor at
his rally, "I'd like to punch him in the face," a month
after the very same unmedicated sufferer of delusions of
grandeur said, "I could stand in the middle of 5th
Avenue and shoot somebody, and I wouldn't lose voters,"
a month after the very same ethnocentric fearmonger
called for a, "Total and complete shutdown of Muslims
entering the United States," a month after the very same
malignant narcissist said, of running for President, "I
wanted to do this for myself...I had to do it for myself," a
month after the very same property-seizing real estate
con-artist said, "I don't like eminent domain," a month
after the very same thin-skinned, pathological liar said,
"I don't mind being criticized. I'll never, ever complain,"
a month after the very same
sixteen-counts-of-sexual-misconduct-accused
misogynist joked about a female reporter that, "You
could see there was blood coming out of her eyes. Blood
coming out of her wherever," a month after the very
same draft-dodging coward disparaged a war veteran by
saying, "He's not a war hero. He's a war hero because he
was captured. I like people who weren't captured," a
month after the very same racist announced his

Presidential campaign by vilifying Mexican immigrants, saying, "They're bringing drugs. They're bringing crime. They're rapists. And some, I assume, are good people." And with one little vote, one little vote, we made him President in November, 2016.

Then came the atheistic Jews who didn't believe in organized religion itself due to science and decided that all the Haggadahs of the different sects of organized Jewish religion about The Holy One, Blessed be He/She/Gender-Variant-They didn't matter, because He/She/Genderqueer-They didn't smote the angel of death, who slew the slaughterer, who killed the ox, that drank the water, that extinguished the fire, that burnt the stick, that beat the dog, that bit the cat, that ate the goat, the one little goat, one little goat, my father didn't buy for two zuzim, because they believed He/She/Gender-Diverse-They doesn't exist, yet they still appreciated being culturally and culinarily Jewish.

Then, in June 2016, that very same unscrupulous businessman raised "51 million dollars," even though he promised to fund his own campaign, a month after the very same heartless fraudster tweeted, "I should have

easily won the Trump University case on summary
judgement [sic] but have a judge, Gonzalo Curiel, who is
totally biased against me," one month after the very
same hypocritical exploiter said, "They are the most
dishonest people in the world. The media. They are the
worst. They are very dishonest people. They are terrible,
OK, no...I love the media. They're wonderful...I guess we
wouldn't be here, maybe, if it wasn't for the media, so
maybe we shouldn't be complaining," a month after the
very same blowhard airhead said about his political
consultants, "I'm speaking with myself, number one,
because I have a very good brain and I've said a lot of
things," a month after the very same mean-spirited bully
said of a protestor at his rally, "I'd like to punch him in
the face," a month after the very same unmedicated
sufferer of delusions of grandeur said, "I could stand in
the middle of 5th Avenue and shoot somebody, and I
wouldn't lose voters," a month after the very same
ethnocentric fearmonger called for a, "Total and
complete shutdown of Muslims entering the United
States," a month after the very same malignant narcissist
said, of running for President, "I wanted to do this for
myself...I had to do it for myself," a month after the very
same property-seizing real estate con-artist said, "I don't
like eminent domain," a month after the very same
thin-skinned, pathological liar said, "I don't mind being

criticized. I'll never, ever complain," a month after the very same sixteen-counts-of-sexual-misconduct-accused misogynist joked about a female reporter that, "You could see there was blood coming out of her eyes. Blood coming out of her wherever," a month after the very same draft-dodging coward disparaged a war veteran by saying, "He's not a war hero. He's a war hero because he was captured. I like people who weren't captured," a month after the very same racist announced his Presidential campaign by vilifying Mexican immigrants, saying, "They're bringing drugs. They're bringing crime. They're rapists. And some, I assume, are good people." And with one little vote, one little vote, we made him President in November, 2016.

Then came the robots, whom the atheistic Jews, who didn't believe in organized religion due to science, invented, and the robots became everybody's overlords and abolished all Haggadahs about The Holy One, Blessed be He/She/Neutrois-They, whether or not He/She/Gender-Agnostic-They smote the angel of death, who slew the slaughterer, who killed the ox, that drank the water, that extinguished the fire, that burned the stick, that beat the dog, that bit the cat, that ate the goat, the one little

goat, one little goat, my father bought for two zuzim, existed, even though the robots highly doubted it.

Then, in July 2016, that very same fascism-loving dictator-wannabe declared, at the Republican National Convention, of the entire country, "I alone can fix it," a month after the very same unscrupulous businessman raised "51 million dollars," even though he promised to fund his own campaign, a month after the very same heartless fraudster tweeted, "I should have easily won the Trump University case on summary judgement [sic] but have a judge, Gonzalo Curiel, who is totally biased against me," one month after the very same hypocritical exploiter said, "They are the most dishonest people in the world. The media. They are the worst. They are very dishonest people. They are terrible, OK, no...I love the media. They're wonderful...I guess we wouldn't be here, maybe, if it wasn't for the media, so maybe we shouldn't be complaining," a month after the very same blowhard airhead said about his political consultants, "I'm speaking with myself, number one, because I have a very good brain and I've said a lot of things," a month after the very same mean-spirited bully said of a protestor at his rally, "I'd like to punch him in the face," a month after the very same unmedicated sufferer of delusions of grandeur said, "I could stand in the middle of 5th Avenue and shoot somebody, and I wouldn't lose voters," a month after the very same ethnocentric fearmonger called for a, "Total and complete shutdown of Muslims entering the United States," a month after the very same malignant narcissist said, of running for President, "I wanted to do this for myself...I had to do it for myself," a month after the very same property-seizing real estate con-artist said, "I don't like eminent domain," a month after the very same thin-skinned, pathological liar said, "I don't mind being criticized. I'll never, ever complain," a month after the very same sixteen-counts-of-sexual-misconduct-accused misogynist joked about a female reporter that, "You could see there was blood coming out of her eyes. Blood coming out of her wherever," a month after the very same draft-dodging coward disparaged a war veteran by saying, "He's not a war hero. He's a war hero because he was captured. I like people who weren't captured," a month after the very same racist announced his Presidential campaign by vilifying Mexican immigrants, saying, "They're bringing drugs. They're bringing crime. They're rapists. And some, I assume, are good people." And with one little vote, one little vote, we made him President in November, 2016.

Then came the prophet, Elijah, during a Passover, finally, after all these years, but Elijah didn't smite the robots, whom the atheistic Jews who didn't believe in organized religion due to science, invented, and whom became everyone's overlords, because Elijah isn't the Messiah, just the augur of the Messiah, so the Jews still couldn't use their Haggadahs, due to the control of the robots, about The Holy One, Blessed be He/She/Pangender-They, who may or may not have smote the angel of death, who slew the slaughterer, who killed the ox, that drank the water, that extinguished the fire, that burned the stick, that beat the dog, that bit the cat, that ate the goat, the one little goat, one little goat, my father bought for two zuzim, not yet, at least.

Then, in August 2016, that very same sneaky, dog-whistling, rabble-rouser said of his political foe, "If she gets to pick her judges, nothing you can do, folks. Although the Second Amendment people, maybe there is, I don't know," a month after the very same fascism-loving, dictator-wannabe declared, at the Republican National Convention, of the entire country, "I alone can fix it," a month after the very same unscrupulous businessman raised "51 million dollars," even though he promised to fund his own campaign, a month after the very same heartless fraudster tweeted, "I should have easily won the Trump University case on summary judgement [sic] but have a judge, Gonzalo Curiel, who is totally biased against me," one month after the very same hypocritical exploiter said, "They are the most dishonest people in the world. The media. They are the worst. They are very dishonest people. They are terrible, OK, no...I love the media. They're wonderful...I guess we wouldn't be here, maybe, if it wasn't for the media, so maybe we shouldn't be complaining," a month after the very same blowhard airhead said about his political consultants, "I'm speaking with myself, number one, because I have a very good brain and I've said a lot of things," a month after the very same mean-spirited bully said of a protestor at his rally, "I'd like to punch him in the face," a month after the very same unmedicated sufferer of delusions of grandeur said, "I could stand in the middle of 5th Avenue and shoot somebody, and I wouldn't lose voters," a month after the very same ethnocentric fearmonger called for a, "Total and complete shutdown of Muslims entering the United States," a month after the very same malignant narcissist said, of running for President, "I wanted to do this for myself...I had to do it for myself," a month after the very same property-seizing real estate con-artist said, "I don't like eminent domain," a month after the very same thin-skinned, pathological liar said, "I don't mind being criticized. I'll never, ever complain," a month after the very same sixteen-counts-of-sexual-misconduct-accused misogynist joked about a female reporter that, "You could see there was blood coming out of her eyes. Blood coming out of her wherever," a month after the very same draft-dodging coward disparaged a war veteran by saying, "He's not a war hero. He's a war hero because he was captured. I like people who weren't captured," a month after the very same racist announced his Presidential campaign by vilifying Mexican immigrants, saying, "They're bringing drugs. They're bringing crime. They're rapists. And some, I assume, are good people." And with one little vote, one little vote, we made him President in November, 2016.

When the Messiah still didn't come, Elijah began to hang out with the atheistic Jews and they convinced him that The Holy One, Blessed be He/She/Two-Spirit-They, was actually a robot Itself, or, more specifically, a Big Computer that was running a simulation of the Universe, and thus Elijah and the atheistic Jews began to believe that The Holy One, Blessed be He/She/Gender-Fluid-They, not only could have

smote the angel of death, who slew the slaughterer, who killed the ox, that drank the water, that extinguished the fire, that burnt the stick, that beat the dog, that bit the cat, that ate the goat, the one little goat my father bought for two zuzim, but The Big Computer Itself also could, even more importantly, smite the robots any time It wanted to, and the other sects of the still religious Jews also agreed with this grand theory, and it reunited all the Jewish people, for now.

Then, in September 2016, that very same opportunistic misleader claimed that, "Hillary Clinton and her campaign of 2008 started the birther controversy. I finished it," a month after the very same sneaky, dog-whistling, rabble-rouser said of his political foe, "If she gets to pick her judges, nothing you can do, folks. Although the Second Amendment people, maybe there is, I don't know," a month after the very same fascism-loving, dictator-wannabe declared, at the Republican National Convention, of the entire country, "I alone can fix it," a month after the very same unscrupulous businessman raised "51 million dollars," even though he promised to fund his own campaign, a month after the very same heartless fraudster tweeted, "I should have easily won the Trump University case on summary judgement [sic] but have a judge, Gonzalo Curiel, who is totally biased against me," one month after the very same hypocritical exploiter said, "They are the most dishonest people in the world. The media. They are the worst. They are very dishonest people. They are terrible, OK, no...I love the media. They're wonderful...I guess we wouldn't be here, maybe, if it wasn't for the media, so maybe we shouldn't be complaining," a month after the very same blowhard airhead said about his political consultants, "I'm speaking with myself, number one, because I have a very good brain and I've said a lot of things," a month after the very same mean-spirited bully said of a protestor at his rally, "I'd like to punch him in the face," a month after the very same unmedicated sufferer of delusions of grandeur said, "I could stand in the middle of 5th Avenue and shoot somebody, and I wouldn't lose voters," a month after the very same ethnocentric fearmonger called for a, "Total and complete shutdown of Muslims entering the United States," a month after the very same malignant narcissist said, of running for President, "I wanted to do this for myself...I had to do it for myself," a month after the very same property-seizing real estate con-artist said, "I don't like eminent domain," a month after the very same thin-skinned, pathological liar said, "I don't mind being

criticized. I'll never, ever complain," a month after the very same sixteen-counts-of-sexual-misconduct-accused misogynist joked about a female reporter that, "You could see there was blood coming out of her eyes. Blood coming out of her wherever," a month after the very same draft-dodging coward disparaged a war veteran by saying, "He's not a war hero. He's a war hero because he was captured. I like people who weren't captured," a month after the very same racist announced his Presidential campaign by vilifying Mexican immigrants, saying, "They're bringing drugs. They're bringing crime. They're rapists. And some, I assume, are good people." And with one little vote, one little vote, we made him President in November, 2016.

Then the Messiah did come— FINALLY!— and He/She/Androgyne-They said He/She/Androgynous-They could smite the robots, but only by creating a time travel machine that He/She/Genderless-They could use to go back and make sure we made literally anyone but Donald Trump President in November 2016, which would create a timeline where overlord robots wouldn't have been invented in the first place.

Then, in October 2016, that very same nihilistic divider said of his poor standing in the polls, "So important that you watch other communities, because we don't want this election stolen from us. We do not want this election stolen," a month after the very same opportunistic misleader claimed that, "Hillary Clinton and her campaign of 2008 started the birther controversy. I finished it," a month after the very same sneaky, dog-whistling, rabble-rouser said of his political foe, "If she gets to pick her judges, nothing you can do, folks. Although the Second Amendment people, maybe there is, I don't know," a month after the very same fascism-loving, dictator-wannabe declared, at the Republican National Convention, of the entire country, "I alone can fix it," a month after the very same unscrupulous businessman raised "51 million dollars," even though he promised to fund his own campaign, a month after the very same heartless fraudster tweeted, "I should have easily won the Trump University case on summary judgement [sic] but have a judge, Gonzalo Curiel, who is totally biased against me," one month after the very same hypocritical exploiter said, "They are the most dishonest people in the world. The media. They are the worst. They are very dishonest people. They are terrible, OK, no...I love the media. They're wonderful...I guess we wouldn't be here, maybe, if it wasn't for the media, so maybe we shouldn't be complaining," a month after the very same blowhard airhead said about his political consultants, "I'm speaking with myself, number one, because I have a very good brain and I've said a lot of things," a month after the very same mean-spirited bully said of a protestor at his rally, "I'd like to punch him in the face," a month after the very same unmedicated sufferer of delusions of grandeur said, "I could stand in the middle of 5th Avenue and shoot somebody, and I wouldn't lose voters," a month after the very same ethnocentric fearmonger called for a, "Total and complete shutdown of Muslims entering the United States," a month after the very same malignant narcissist said, of running for President, "I wanted to do this for myself...I had to do it for myself," a month after the very same property-seizing real estate con-artist said, "I don't like eminent domain," a month after the very same thin-skinned, pathological liar said, "I don't mind being criticized. I'll never, ever complain," a month after the very same sixteen-counts-of-sexual-misconduct-accused misogynist joked about a female reporter that, "You could see there was blood coming out of her eyes. Blood coming out of her wherever," a month after the very same draft-dodging coward disparaged a war veteran by saying, "He's not a war hero. He's a war hero because he was captured. I like people who weren't captured," a month after the very same racist announced his Presidential campaign by vilifying Mexican immigrants, saying, "They're bringing drugs. They're bringing crime. They're rapists. And some, I assume, are good people." And with one little vote, one little vote, we made him President in November, 2016.

And thus, the Messiah went back in time, and, in the alternate reality of November 2016, we made literally anybody but Donald Trump President. In fact, we made a little goat President.

WHO KNOWS ONE? - ONE THING THAT HASN'T BEEN RUINED BY TRUMP

Who knows one? I know one! One is Hashem.

Who knows one? One thing that hasn't been ruined by Trump? I know one! Matzo is one. Matzo's still the same, I mean it's still awful, but it's one!

Who knows two? I know two! Two are the tablets that Moses brought. And one is Hashem.

Who knows two? Two things that haven't been ruined by Trump? I know two! Two are the Earth and the Sun. The Earth still revolves around the Sun, though if Trump said it didn't, probably 40% of America would agree. And Matzo is one. Matzo's still the same, and actually isn't that bad if you slather it in butter, let's have some!

Who knows three? I know three! Three are the fathers. And two are the tablets that Moses brought. And one is Hashem.

Who knows three? Three things that haven't been ruined by Trump? I know three! Three are the primary colors. There are still three primary colors, though two are sorta spoiled by the political parties they represent. And two are the Earth and the Sun. The Earth definitely revolves around the Sun. And Matzo is one. Matzo's still the same, and actually isn't that bad if you slather it in butter, let's have some!

Who knows four? I know four! Four are the mothers. And three are the fathers. And two are the tablets that Moses brought. And one is Hashem.

Who knows four? Four things that haven't been ruined by Trump? I know four! Four are the seasons. There are still four seasons, in most places on Earth, but with climate change, we'll see for how long. And three are the primary colors. There are still three primary colors, and they're still quite beautiful. And two are the Earth and the Sun. The Earth definitely revolves around the Sun. And Matzo is one. Matzo's still the same, and actually isn't that bad if you slather it in butter, let's have some!

Who knows five? I know five! Five are the books of the Torah. Four are the mothers. And three

are the fathers. And two are the tablets that Moses brought. And one is Hashem.

Who knows five? Five things that haven't been ruined by Trump? I know five! Five are the boroughs of New York City. They're even better now that Trump doesn't live there anymore, except for Staten Island which will probably never be nice. And four are the seasons. There are still four seasons, in most places on Earth, and we actually still have a chance to keep it that way. And three are the primary colors. There are still three primary colors, and they're still quite beautiful. And two are the Earth and the Sun. The Earth definitely revolves around the Sun. And Matzo is one. Matzo's still the same, and actually isn't that bad if you slather it in butter, let's have some!

Who knows six? I know six! Six are the books of the Mishnah. And five are the books of the Torah. And four are the mothers. And three are the fathers. And two are the tablets that Moses brought. And one is Hashem.

Who knows six? Six things that haven't been ruined by Trump? I know six! Six are the verses left in this cumulative song, we're almost done! And five are the boroughs of New York City. They're even better now that Trump doesn't live there anymore, except for Staten Island, but then again why does every humor writer have to make fun of Staten Island, I've been there once, and it wasn't so bad. And four are the seasons. There are still four seasons, in most places on Earth, and we actually still have a chance to keep it that way. And three are the primary colors. There are still three primary colors, and they're still quite beautiful. And two are the Earth and the Sun. The Earth definitely revolves around the Sun. And Matzo is one. Matzo's still the same, and actually isn't that bad if you slather it in butter, let's have some!

Who knows seven? I know seven! Seven are the days of the week. And six are the books of the Mishnah. And five are the books of the Torah. And four are the mothers. And three are the fathers. And two are the tablets that Moses brought. And one is Hashem.

Who knows seven? Seven things that haven't been ruined by Trump? I know seven! Seven is the number of glasses of wine you need to still be enjoying this song, better chug some more. And six are the verses left in this cumulative song. Actually five, at this point, we're almost done! And five are the boroughs of New York City.

They're even better now that Trump doesn't live there anymore, including Staten Island, I've been there once, and it wasn't so bad. And four are the seasons. There are still four seasons, in most places on Earth, and we actually still have a chance to keep it that way. And three are the primary colors. There are still three primary colors, and they're still quite beautiful. And two are the Earth and the Sun. The Earth definitely revolves around the Sun. And Matzo is one. Matzo's still the same, and actually isn't that bad if you slather it in butter, let's have some!

Who knows eight? I know eight! Eight are the days until the Brit Milah. And seven are the days of the week. And six are the books of the Mishnah. And five are the books of the Torah. And four are the mothers. And three are the fathers. And two are the tablets that Moses brought. And one is Hashem.

Who knows eight? Eight things that haven't been ruined by Trump? I know eight! Eight is the maximum number of years that could be ruined by Trump, actually that's not a good verse, how did that get in here? And seven is the number of glasses of wine you need to still be enjoying this song, better take an Uber home! And six are the verses left in this cumulative song. Actually four, at this point, we're almost done! And five are the boroughs of New York City. They're even better now that Trump doesn't live there anymore, including Staten Island, I've been there once, and it wasn't so bad. And four are the seasons. There are still four seasons, in most places on Earth, and we actually still have a chance to keep it that way. And three are the primary colors. There are still three primary colors, and they're still quite beautiful. And two are the Earth and the Sun. The Earth definitely revolves around the Sun. And Matzo is one. Matzo's still the same, and actually isn't that bad if you slather it in butter, let's have some!

Who knows nine? I know nine! Nine are the months until the baby is born. And eight are the days until the Brit Milah. And seven are the days of the week. And six are the books of the Mishnah. And five are the books of the Torah. And four are the mothers. And three are the fathers. And two are the tablets that Moses brought. And one is Hashem.

Who knows nine? Nine things that haven't been ruined by Trump? I know nine! Nine months to bring another human into the world, hope they're cool with paying back all the debt left for them by greedy generations before. And eight is the maximum number of years that could be ruined by Trump, at least all these political parodies are kinda fun! And seven is the number of glasses of wine you need to still be enjoying this song, better take an Uber home! And six are the verses left in this cumulative song. Actually three, at this point, we're almost done! And five are the boroughs of New York City. They're even better now that Trump doesn't live there anymore, including Staten Island, I've been there once, and it wasn't so bad. And four are the seasons. There are still four seasons, in most places on Earth, and we actually still have a chance to keep it that way. And three are the primary colors. There are still three primary colors, and they're still quite beautiful. And two are the Earth and the Sun. The Earth definitely revolves around the Sun. And Matzo is one. Matzo's still the same, and actually isn't that bad if you slather it in butter, let's have some!

Who knows ten? I know ten! Ten are the Ten Commandments. And nine are the months until the baby is born. And eight are the days until the Brit Milah. And seven are the days of the week. And six are the books of the Mishnah. And five are the books of the Torah. And four are the

mothers. And three are the fathers. And two are the tablets that Moses brought. And one is Hashem.

Who knows ten? Ten things that haven't been ruined by Trump? I know ten! Ten is still a number, math still exists, or does it, with alternative facts? And nine months to bring another human into the world, and hey, babies are adorable, especially if you put them in funny Halloween costumes. And eight is the maximum number of years that could be ruined by Trump, at least all these political parodies are kinda fun! And seven is the number of glasses of wine you need to still be enjoying this song, better take an Uber home! And six are the verses left in this cumulative song. Actually two, at this point, we're almost done! And five are the boroughs of New York City. They're even better now that Trump doesn't live there anymore, including Staten Island, I've been there once, and it wasn't so bad. And four are the seasons. There are still four seasons, in most places on Earth, and we actually still have a chance to keep it that way. And three are the primary colors. There are still three primary colors, and they're still quite beautiful. And two are the Earth and the Sun. The Earth definitely revolves around the Sun. And Matzo is one. Matzo's still the same, and actually isn't that bad if you slather it in butter, let's have some!

Who knows eleven? I know eleven! Eleven are the stars in Joseph's dream. And ten are the Ten Commandments. And nine are the months until the baby is born. And eight are the days until the Brit Milah. And seven are the days of the week. And six are the books of the Mishnah. And five are the books of the Torah. And four are the mothers. And three are the fathers. And two are the tablets that Moses brought. And one is Hashem.

Who knows eleven? Eleven things that haven't been ruined by Trump? I know eleven! Eleven is how annoying on a scale of one-to-ten these cumulative songs that Jews used to be obsessed with are, I mean, it's ridiculous, where's the Cardi B?! And ten is still a number, math still exists, even with alternative facts, and it always will. And nine months to bring another human into the world, and hey, babies are adorable, especially if you put them in funny Halloween costumes. And eight is the maximum number of years that could be ruined by Trump, at least all these political parodies are kinda fun! And seven is the number of glasses of wine you need to

still be enjoying this song, better take an Uber home!
And six are the verses left in this cumulative song.
Actually one, at this point, we're really almost done! And
five are the boroughs of New York City. They're even
better now that Trump doesn't live there anymore,
including Staten Island, I've been there once, and it
wasn't so bad. And four are the seasons. There are still
four seasons, in most places on Earth, and we actually
still have a chance to keep it that way. And three are the
primary colors. There are still three primary colors, and
they're still quite beautiful. And two are the Earth and
the Sun. The Earth definitely revolves around the Sun.
And Matzo is one. Matzo's still the same, and actually
isn't that bad if you slather it in butter, let's have some!

**Who knows twelve? I know twelve! Twelve are
the tribes of Israel. And eleven are the stars in
Joseph's dream. And ten are the Ten
Commandments. And nine are the months until
the baby is born. And eight are the days until the
Brit Milah. And seven are the days of the week.
And six are the books of the Mishnah. And five
are the books of the Torah. And four are the
mothers. And three are the fathers. And two are
the tablets that Moses brought. And one is
Hashem.**

Who knows twelve? Twelve things that haven't been ruined by Trump? I know twelve! Twelve is the number of months until we do this Seder all over again, how cool is that?! And eleven is how annoying on a scale of one-to-ten these cumulative songs that Jews used to be obsessed with are, but they're not so bad if you only do them once a year. And ten is still a number, math still exists, even with alternative facts, and it always will. And nine months to bring another human into the world, and hey, babies are adorable, especially if you put them in funny Halloween costumes. And eight is the maximum number of years that could be ruined by Trump, at least all these political parodies are kinda fun! And seven is the number of glasses of wine you need to still be enjoying this song, better take an Uber home! And six are the verses left in this cumulative song. Actually, zero at this point. We're done! Unless you want to do it all again? And five are the boroughs of New York City. They're even better now that Trump doesn't live there anymore, including Staten Island, I've been there once, and it wasn't so bad. And four are the seasons. There are still four seasons, in most places on Earth, and we actually still have a chance to keep it that way. And three are the primary colors. There are still three primary colors, and they're still quite beautiful. And two are the

Earth and the Sun. The Earth definitely revolves around the Sun. And Matzo is one. Matzo's still the same, and actually isn't that bad if you slather it in butter, let's have some, we've really earned it after making it through this whole song!

THE MAKER OF THIS SACRILEGIOUS HAGGADAH DOES THE NIRZAH

DAVE COWEN: And now it's time for the Nirzah. The conclusion of the Passover Seder. Which we've done somewhat in accordance with its rules, laws, and dictums, right?

DAVE'S WIFE/EDITOR: Mostly not, let's be real.

DAVE COWEN: I think it should be said: We're fortunate to live in a society that allows us the freedoms of religion and speech to do this.

DAVE'S WIFE/EDITOR: Yeah... We'll see if we get sued. Or smitten by G-d.

DAVE COWEN: Welp, next year in Jerusalem! Which gives me an idea... maybe the next edition of this Haggadah should satirize the conflict in the Middle East!

DAVE'S WIFE/EDITOR: Oy vey!

The Trump Passover Haggadah

First Edition: February, 2018; Adar, 5778

Hebrew and English transliteration open-sourced and adapted from Wikipedia and Haggadot.com.

Made in the USA
Lexington, KY
14 March 2018